BRITAIN'S 🏰 HERITAGE

The Fifties Railway

Greg Morse

AMBERLEY

Acknowledgements

I am indebted to Roger Badger, Derek Hotchkiss, Philip Hunt, Julia Jenkins, Gerald Riley, Debbie Stevens, Michael Woods and Nick Wright.

My thanks also go to those who supplied many of the images in this book: Colour-Rail (incorporating the work of E. Alger, the C. Banks Collection, C. C. B. Herbert, David Lawrence, R. J. Maxwell and E. Oldham), Rail Photoprints (Hugh Ballantyne, Alan H. Bryant ARPS, John Day Collection, the David Cobbe Collection, the Ray Hinton Archive, Martin Hunt, Gordon Edgar, Sid Rickard, R. A. Whitfield and R. S. Wilkins), the Swindon Library Collection and STEAM Museum, Swindon.

Cover: Castle Class No. 5090 *Neath Abbey* enters Bristol Temple Meads with the empty stock for the Up 'Bristolian' on 3 June 1959. (Rail Photoprints/David Cobbe Collection)

First published 2018

Amberley Publishing
The Hill, Stroud
Gloucestershire, GL5 4EP

www.amberley-books.com

Copyright © Greg Morse, 2018

The right of Greg Morse to be identified as the Author of this work has been asserted in accordance with the Copyrights, Designs and Patents Act 1988.

ISBN 978 1 4456 7919 8 (paperback)
ISBN 978 1 4456 7920 4 (ebook)

British Library Cataloguing in Publication Data.
A catalogue record for this book is available from the British Library.

Printed in the UK.

Contents

1

Introduction – All Change for Nationalisation?

Bottle green. That's what you'll remember in the long years ahead. A bottle green coat and a hat to match. You saw her pass, saw the car that took her on her tour of the borough. Fifty in 1950. That's what Swindon was. A queen in waiting. That's what Princess Elizabeth was (though none could have known it that wet autumn morning). Bottle green. The colour of the engines built in the town. Almost.

You leave the streets lined with flag-wavers, well-wishers young and old, and head to the great Works, home of the Great Western: God's Wonderful Railway. After lunch you join the crowd within, nudging your way to the front to watch: to watch with your fellows, you who had built this machine, you who'd formed the boiler, fitted the frame, forged the firebox, turned the pistons. You who'd spent hours of effort – hours of skill – to make her ready: a vision of beauty, copper-capped chimney shining, a curtain veiling seven letters of brass.

The gloved hand of royalty pulls the cord to reveal those seven letters to spell *Swindon*, the engine now named after the place of its birth, whose coat of arms stands proud on the splasher below. There is applause. There is joy – sadness too, for this is the last. The last of the line. The last Castle. You all knew it was, but couldn't know that in just ten years there'd be another ceremony for the last steam engine of all. Not that the Great Western hadn't been looking forward: it'd considered main line electrification twice, been quick to enter into the oil firing experiment in a bid to save coal – and money – after the war, and been keen to

HRH Princess Elizabeth at Swindon on 15 November 1950, in the cab not of *Swindon* – the locomotive she named that day – but No. 4057, a Star class engine also called *Princess Elizabeth*.

No. 7037 *Swindon* at its namesake depot. It was the last Castle class to be built, though the Works which bore it would also produce the last steam locomotive to be built for British Railways, a Standard class 9F, which would be released to traffic in March 1960.

explore other forms of traction. This manifested itself first in another Castle – 'Kerosene Castle', the nickname given to a gas turbine-powered locomotive built for the GWR by Brown-Boveri of Switzerland. The trouble was the GWR would be the Western Region of British Railways by the time it had been delivered. The Great Way Round had gone with regret, gone forever.

* * * * * *

Swindon was named at Swindon Works on 15 November 1950, almost three years after the 1947 Transport Act had brought the Great Western, London Midland & Scottish, London & North Eastern and Southern railways (along with fifty smaller concerns) into public ownership. To mark the move, locomotive whistles up and down the land had cut through the darkness at midnight on 31 December. As they headed to work in the early hours of 1948, some staff had feared for the future; others felt more optimistic; many 'old school' managers vowed to do as they'd always done while the 'top brass' reorganised itself.

The system had been divided into six regions (the Eastern, London Midland, North Eastern, Scottish, Southern, and Western), above which sat an executive, one of five that

Did you know?

The GWR received parliamentary approval for a line between Bristol and London in August 1835, the same being granted to the Cheltenham & Great Western Union the following June. The Chief Engineer for these works was Isambard Kingdom Brunel, who soon set about acquiring locomotives from various sources. This, alas, resulted in a locomotive roster of somewhat mixed quality. In 1837, Brunel recruited Daniel Gooch and charged him with rectifying the heavy repair burden thus created. Gooch chose a greenfield site at Swindon, as it marked the point where the gentler gradients of the Thames Valley gave way to the more arduous terrain through Box and Bath. If a 'principal engine establishment' were here, he argued, loco changes to and from the more powerful classes needed for the western half of the run could be made with ease. As it would be necessary to have some form of installation at Swindon for the Cheltenham traffic anyway, Gooch reasoned that it made sense to centralise. Brunel and the Board agreed. Construction began in 1841, Swindon Works becoming operational on 2 January 1843.

Swindon Works and its Place in British Railway History was published by the Western Region in 1950, just after Princess Elizabeth's visit. The cover shows a King class locomotive undergoing repair.

BRITISH RAILWAYS

BROAD
OUTLINE
OF REGIONS

SCOTTISH

NORTH
EASTERN

LONDON
MIDLAND

EASTERN

WESTERN

SOUTHERN

SOUTHERN
WESTERN

A map produced by BR in 1948, showing its original six regions. These would become five from 1 January 1967, when the North Eastern was absorbed into the Eastern.

answered to the British Transport Commission. The latter had been established to provide 'an efficient, adequate, economical and properly integrated system of public inland transport and port facilities within Great Britain for passengers and goods'. Thus its first chairman, professional civil servant Sir Cyril Hurcomb, oversaw executives that controlled not only the railway, but also bus companies, road hauliers, docks, hotels, canals, tramways, shipping lines, London Transport, and even a film unit.

Trading as 'British Railways' (BR), the Railway Executive inherited over 20,000 locomotives, 56,000 coaches, a million wagons, 43,000 road vehicles and almost 9,000 horses. But while the exigencies of war meant many of these assets were well past their best, the industry

DARLINGTON

BR's new 'totems' soon started to appear on signs and stationery. Each region was allotted a distinctive colour: the Southern had green, the Western brown, London Midland maroon, the Scottish Region light blue and the Eastern dark blue. The North Eastern, however, received this rather startling shade of tangerine.

No. 5098 *Clifford Castle* takes the Up 'Cornishman' past Cowley Bridge, Exeter – a classic early '50s scene.

was as vital to the country as it ever had been. As a 'common carrier', BR could refuse no consignment, so sitting at your breakfast table in Bristol, Brighton, Cardiff or Dundee, the newspaper in front of you, the coal in the grate, the early morning post – even that oil painting from Uncle Fred – still came by train, at least part of the way. It was the same with holidays and business trips – air travel was only for the rich; so was car ownership (though even those who did have a car probably wouldn't have had enough coupons to fill the tank for a long journey anyway).

Big stations could be sooty, pre-war carriages tatty, trains overcrowded, slow and bumpy, but there was little litter, and staff were attentive. Changing mid-journey for a branch line in Somerset or Suffolk, say, you might have had time to repair to a cosy waiting room, where an idle moment could be enjoyed as the train puffed in from its secluded rural terminus. Taking a seat in an empty compartment at last, you might muse – all things considered – that the fifties railway wasn't so very different from the forties railway, the thirties railway or even the twenties one. The GWR hadn't really gone at all. Neither had the LMS, LNER or Southern, in this world of Terence Cuneo paintings and Reverend Awdry stories, where the warmth of the familiar was breathing on regardless. And yet...

2
Man of Steam

It's *so* annoying. What nonsense are they going to come out with next? The trouble with these new brooms is that they think they can solve the world's problems inside a couple of meetings. Maybe in some industries they can. Perhaps there, the able, classically schooled civil servant is a positive boon. But not in railways. Railways are a foreign country. Things are done differently.

It was a cynical view, perhaps. Some might call it obstructive. Yet you know you aren't alone, and as you arrive at 'The Kremlin' that morning, you see a man who shares it. You doff your hat. He doffs his. You both go in. It is the custom...

The building – 222 Marylebone Road – got its nickname from its labyrinth of corridors and passageways. First a hotel, then a hostel for trainmen, it's now the home of the Railway Executive.

Your fellow 'cynic' is of course Robert Arthur Riddles – RE member for locomotive design and construction, who started his career at Crewe in 1909, who went on to become Vice President of the LMS, and who is no stranger to the footplate, having volunteered as a driver during the General Strike and accompanied one of the company's Pacifics on a tour of the States, taking the controls himself for much of the trip. At the Ministry of Supply during the war, he'd been responsible for the acquisition of motive power. He owes his current position to nationalisation. It is not something on which to congratulate him entirely, given the complexity of his task.

Stanier Pacific No. 46229 *Duchess of Hamilton* passes Frodsham Junction with the diverted Up 'Royal Scot' *c.* 1950. It was this locomotive – disguised as No. 6220 *Coronation* – that Riddles accompanied to the United States in 1939.

Men of the rail, among whom (seated front row, second from the right) is R. A. Riddles, Railway Executive Member for Mechanical and Electrical Engineering, 1948–53.

When Hugh Dalton, Labour Chancellor of the Exchequer, described the RE's inheritance as 'a very poor bag of physical assets', it had been almost impossible to disagree. Some of the tank engines in use on former Southern and LNER branches, for example, were in such bad shape that new LMS-designed locomotives had to be drafted in to cover the timetable, locomotives from the team led by H. G. Ivatt, who'd taken over as that company's Chief Mechanical Engineer after the untimely death of his predecessor – Charles Fairburn – in 1945. Now 'CME' of naught but the London Midland Region of British Railways, like Fairburn, Ivatt had been an advocate of the internal combustion engine, but where the former had been actively involved in the introduction of diesel-powered shunting engines, it would be the latter that oversaw the introduction of No. 10000, a fully fledged 1,600 hp diesel-electric.

Built with English Electric equipment at Derby Works, this shining machine had been presented to the press in December 1947. Making a trial run to Watford later that month, it marked – for EE's publicity department, at least – a 'new page' in locomotive development. It was soon seen surging over the metals, and soon joined by a twin (No. 10001), the pair often working in multiple on expresses out of Euston. By December 1950, the two had multiplied to six as an 827 hp diesel-electric (No. 10800), a diesel-mechanical co-designed by Col. L. F. R. Fell (No. 10100), and two 1,750 hp units part-designed by Oliver Bulleid (Nos 10201–2) took to the rails. The LNER had invited tenders for twenty-five diesel-electrics to replace thirty-two of its mighty Pacifics back in 1947; this valiant hope, however, had been dashed by the RE with some speed after nationalisation.

Above: No. 62231 shows off its early BR livery at Keith. The engine was a member of the D41 class, whose pedigree reached back to 1893, when the first of its type was introduced by the Great North of Scotland Railway.

Below: A modern LMS tank engine, in the form of Ivatt class 2 No. 41206, seen arriving at Skipton with a local service *c.* 1950.

Former LMS diesel-electric No. 10000 passes a 4-SUB electric multiple unit near Wimbledon. The former's train features the new 'Standard' BR carriages (soon to be re-dubbed 'Mark I').

Did you know?

Often at odds with Riddles, Oliver Bulleid had become CME of the Southern Railway in 1937. Though famed for his steam locomotives, he played an active part in electrification, designing several multiple units and three locomotives (with Chief Electrical Engineer Alfred Raworth).

His last steam locomotive for the SR was the unconventional Leader, which appeared after nationalisation, and whose boiler and tender were housed in a diesel-like double-ended body. Alas, it was not successful, although the diesel-electrics for which he provided the mechanical configuration (Nos 10201–3) did form the basis of BR's later English Electric Type 4s (see pages 48–49).

Having become CME of the Southern Region in 1948, Bulleid left BR two years later to fulfil the same function for Córas Iompair Éireann in Ireland. He retired in 1958, later moving to Malta, where he died in 1970, aged eighty-seven.

Had Ivatt or Bulleid been at the helm, any one of these 'new pages' – real or requested – might have turned more quickly. As it was, Riddles doubted the reliability of the diesel, seeing electrification as the ultimate goal (at least for the main lines). As an apprentice, he'd taken a course in electrical engineering, feeling – rightly – that there'd be a future for electric traction. The trouble was that electrification was clearly a long-term project, and practical solutions were needed quickly.

Though the GWR's Locomotive Committee had discussed the possibilities of main line diesel traction, its decision to experiment with gas turbines (illustrated by No. 18000, which finally appeared in February 1950) shows that the suitability of the internal combustion engine to heavy passenger and freight work was not considered proven by all British engineers and managers in the mid-1940s.

Thankfully, the production lines of some of the major railway workshops were in full swing on a range of pre-nationalisation steam designs. By letting this continue, Riddles could withdraw some of the oldest types on BR's books – like the ex-Great Western 'Bulldog' 4-4-0s (1899–1910) and ex-Great Northern 'Atlantics' (1902–10) – while he developed a suite of uncomplicated classes of his own.

Although no single Big Four locomotive stood head and shoulders above the rest, the resulting twelve types would tend to favour LMS practice. Given the background of Riddles (and his assistants, R. C. Bond and E. S. Cox), this was unsurprising, although LMS engines were known to enjoy a high availability rate and a certain degree of standardisation. The decision to take the Midland path was also shaped (to some extent) by the exchange trials Riddles had initiated in BR's first year, in which engines from each of the Big Four were sent to other regions for assessment. While more useful results would doubtless have been reached in the new testing plant at Rugby (which had opened in October 1948), the exchanges were good publicity and may have helped show locomotive superintendents that 'foreign' classes could perform as well as those they were used to – an important point to make when working on a range of engines for nationwide deployment.

Unfortunately, these trials were also the first the BTC had heard about the RE's traction policy. The Commission believed the various motive power types available should be tested and had written a letter to that effect in April 1948. That the RE had taken eight months to reply – and only then to note that a committee had been established – says something about the relationship between the two bodies. To a point, the problem was about personalities: the RE chairman – Sir Eustace Missenden (erstwhile General Manager of the Southern) – was suspicious of civil servants and politicians, while Hurcomb's diffidence did not endear

Above: The first 'Standard' steam locomotive to be completed was No. 70000 *Britannia*, which emerged from Crewe Works in January 1951. Seen near Belton, it was soon followed by fifty-four classmates.
Below: The next 'Standard' type to emerge was the Class 5MT, which was based on Stanier's 'Black Five' mixed traffic design for the LMS. By the middle of 1957, there would be 172 on BR's books. In this view, No. 73000 glows at Neasden in 1951.

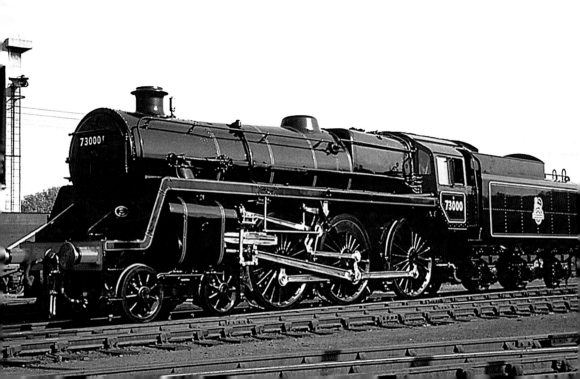

Above: Like Nos 10000–1 and 10201–3, No. 10800 was tested on the London Midland and Southern regions, although it also enjoyed a spell on the Eastern. Ordered by the LMS, the locomotive first appeared in 1950. Later bought and rebuilt by Brush Traction for testing purposes, it remained in active use until 1968.

Below: No. 10100 was an experimental diesel-mechanical locomotive built for its designers by the LMS works at Derby. Being a diesel-mechanical, torque from the engine was conveyed direct to the axles via a gearbox. Sold to BR in 1955, it was withdrawn three years later after a fire at Manchester.

him to professional railwaymen, who – like Riddles – were irritated at having to explain or defend policies to those who knew considerably less about railways than they. For his part, Hurcomb – the intellectually very able former Permanent Secretary of the Ministry of Transport and a man who'd been active in the formation of the '47 Act – was baffled by the RE's staunch independence.

Did you know?

While indeed of clear LMS parentage (albeit with a nod to the Great Western – not least regarding the chimney, which had been designed at Swindon Works), the Britannias incorporated a derivation of the boiler and trailing wheel arrangement used by Bulleid on his famous Merchant Navy class. The firebox featured a rocking grate, which allowed the fire to be rebuilt without stopping the locomotive; a self-cleaning smokebox helped speed up shedding procedures at the end of the day, while the raised running plates and valve gear eased lubrication and maintenance.

Politics aside, the first 'Standard' to be completed was No. 70000 *Britannia*, which emerged from Crewe Works in January 1951. Followed by fifty-four classmates, a marriage of high power and low weight allowed them to revolutionise services, not least on the Eastern

The driver looks on from the imposing form of Bulleid Merchant Navy Pacific No. 35006 *Peninsular & Oriental S. N. Co.* as it waits to leave Sidmouth Junction in 1951.

Region, where they improved the timings that could be achieved between Liverpool Street, Norwich and Cambridge appreciably. London Midland drivers also returned positive reports – particularly on Euston–Holyhead turns – while the Western's general dislike was contradicted by Cardiff's Canton Depot, which put them to good use on South Wales services.

At the time, these expresses – and their secondary and rural counterparts – featured one of the 56,000 vehicles BR had inherited. This meant that, while you might be lucky enough to find yourself heading to a twelve-wheeled dining car of 1930s vintage for Dover Sole (if you had the money), you could also end up bouncing along in a shabby third-class compartment whose fifty-year life had been prolonged by the war. The oldest ('pre-Grouping') types would probably have been 'out in the sticks', most having been cascaded down the ranks as newer stock came on stream. From March, though, something even newer was starting to arrive at certain stations...

The watchword once again had been standardisation, Riddles and his colleagues considering how the Big Four had sought solutions to the same problems before setting about incorporating the best of them into their own designs. But while LMS practice returned to favour – especially in terms of the all-steel construction and the proportions of the bodyside windows – the curved profile owed something to Bulleid's work on the Southern, the coupling type and gangway design echoed LNER practice, while the bogies leaned more heavily towards the Great Western.

Taking a seat in one of these ecumenical vehicles, you may not like the exterior livery of carmine and cream (soon redubbed 'blood and custard' by some), but you might have been more impressed with the simple detailing, the shiny ceiling laminates and wooden wall finishes, impressed too with the smoothness of the ride ... until 60 mph was exceeded, when things could get jerky as the bogies began to oscillate on the rails. Things could get

Designed by Oliver Bulleid and Alfred Raworth for the Southern Railway, electric locomotive No. 20001 appeared in 1941. By 1948, it had been joined by two similar machines, all three of which would give around twenty years' service for BR. Here, 'No. 1' takes a train of Pullman stock through Clapham Junction.

Bulleid-designed diesel-electric No. 10201 did not appear until 1950. Like No. 10202, which appeared in 1951, No. 10201 was capable of 1,750 hp. A 2,000 hp variant was outshopped from Brighton Works in 1954 (see page 30). All three were withdrawn as non-standard at the end of 1963.

noisy too, as the metal bodies had not been sufficiently insulated against sound, unlike their largely wooden predecessors. Still, they did look impressive behind a gleaming Britannia on 'The Red Dragon' or an A4 on 'The Flying Scotsman'. They were also much sturdier than their earlier counterparts. Which was just as well, as it turned out...

3
Safer by Road?

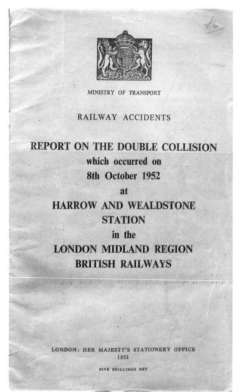

MINISTRY OF TRANSPORT

RAILWAY ACCIDENTS

REPORT ON THE DOUBLE COLLISION
which occurred on
8th October 1952
at
**HARROW AND WEALDSTONE
STATION**
in the
**LONDON MIDLAND REGION
BRITISH RAILWAYS**

LONDON: HER MAJESTY'S STATIONERY OFFICE
1953

FIVE SHILLINGS NET

The report into the Harrow & Wealdstone accident, in which the investigator, Lt-Col. Wilson, noted that while the fatality count had been high, the collision demonstrated the strength of BR's new Mark I carriages, two of which – featuring the latest arrangement of all-steel welded bodies, mounted on 200-ton end-load resistant underframes – were in the ex-Euston train.

Did you know?

The official investigation into Harrow & Wealdstone confirmed that the Perth train had passed a colour-light Distant signal at 'caution' and two semaphore signals at 'danger'. Its author, Lieutenant-Colonel Wilson, urged BR to continue with the 'Warning Control' programme it was developing (and which followed earlier GWR and LMS systems). This was designed to give an audible indication of the status of Distant signals and clearly could have prevented the accident. By 1956, 'Warning Control' (or AWS, the Automatic Warning System) would be fitted between King's Cross and Grantham. In time, it would help reduce the number of fatalities in train accidents significantly.

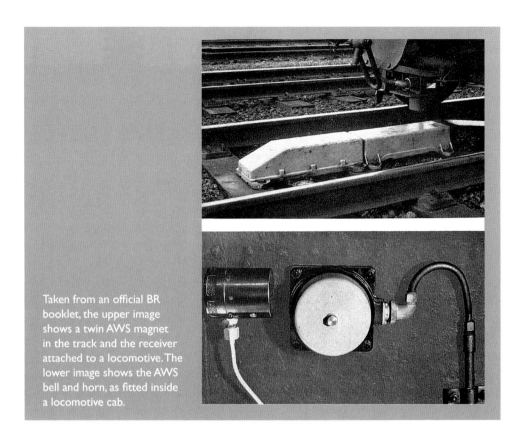

Taken from an official BR booklet, the upper image shows a twin AWS magnet in the track and the receiver attached to a locomotive. The lower image shows the AWS bell and horn, as fitted inside a locomotive cab.

Fog. Always fog. Fog in London. Fog on the Thames. It was bad enough on its own, but when it combined with smoke from factories and the burning fires of home, it became smog and could be lethal. At Harrow & Wealdstone one autumn morning, it hung over the station like a pall. Visibility may have improved as breakfasts were hurriedly consumed and people scurried off to work, but up on the railway it was still less than a hundred yards at the Distant signal. Shortly after 8:15, a commuter train from Tring pulled in and waited. Its nine coaches were packed with 800 passengers; many more were getting ready to board. Some would have only ninety seconds left to live. At 8:19, a 'sleeper' from Perth burst out of the murk, over the points and struck it with such force that the last three coaches were crushed to the length of little more than one, and the whole train was pushed forward some 20 yards.

Although the signalman acted quickly in returning his signals to 'danger', it was too late to stop a Euston–Liverpool/Manchester express, whose engines were making up time after a delay at the terminus, whose engines were powering along at 60 mph. Whose engines were unable to avoid running into the wreckage.

In all, 112 people would be killed, though if you'd been sitting in one of BR's new carriages heading to Stafford or Crewe, your chance of survival would have been heightened by their structural integrity. Not that you'd know that, as your wounds were tended amidst the grim debris (although you'll later agree that the scene was 'like a battlefield', that 'the nation had looked too closely upon horror' in the last decade, that hopes had been tossed like the engines and coaches piled up like so many broken toys). 'In the presence of such disaster,' Pathé News went on, 'we can take no comfort, save in the manner in which our men have acquitted themselves.' The first ambulance and doctor had arrived within three minutes; others soon followed, along with the police, fire brigade and a medical unit from a United States Air Force team based nearby. Help also came from the Salvation Army, the Women's Voluntary Service, local residents and local engineering firms, who lent both staff and equipment. It was harrowing work. It was urgent work. It was necessary work. And they did it, first with hastily improvised bandages, then with stretchers, plasma and splints to help limbs – if not minds – to heal.

By this time, the chairman of the Railway Executive was John Elliot. He was on the scene within the hour. Horrified by what he saw, he would later write that 8 October 1952 was the worst day of his 'railway life'. But who was to blame? The Prime Minister wanted answers. The Prime Minister was Winston Churchill, and Churchill was not a man to be denied. The pressure was great, but Elliot was firm: as chairman, it was ultimately down to him. If the PM must have a name, he told the Transport Minister, 'give him mine'. In the end, it would not be necessary, a simple statement of fact being made to the Commons, as was usual when there'd been a train accident. Not that train accidents were as frequent or fatal as they had been twenty, fifty, sixty years before – though there was an increasing lobby that insisted it was 'safer by road'.

Safer by road. And the banner on the side of the bus proudly says so. A man pays the peak-capped conductor as the driver gets her into gear. Racing down the lanes that leave the village, the bus draws alongside its competition, as it puffs its way through the verdant, bucolic, technicolour landscape. On and on and on and on they go, like something out of a

No. 1467 – an engine similar to that featured in feature film *The Titfield Thunderbolt* (1953) – leaves a snowy Highworth with a service for Swindon Junction in December 1952. Alas, bus competition would see the public timetable to this Wiltshire terminus abolished on 2 March 1953, although workmen's trains would continue to operate for another nine years.

Above: Attention to detail: a sign erected at Camerton, which doubled for Titfield in *The Titfield Thunderbolt*.

Below: Eastern Region-based No. 60908 is an unusual sight as it leaves Surbiton in June 1953 with a service from Waterloo. The loco was one of several V2s loaned to Nine Elms to provide stopgap power following the stopping of all Merchant Navy Pacifics for examination after the Crewkerne incident (see page 26).

A 'push-pull' service waits at Gravesend West on 1 August 1953. Within two days the station will close to passengers, handling only freight until 1968. After the Second World War, traffic here declined as more passengers chose Gravesend Central and its fast electric service.

Reverend Awdry story, bus and train racing, passengers bracing, each out-pacing ... until a bend takes the bus straight into the path of a steam roller. The tank engine's whistle is almost triumphant. 'It's safer by road!' shouts the squire-cum-guard to his hapless rival...

You survey the scene, and laugh. You survey the scene, but not from the roadside. You're sitting in a cinema the following spring. You're watching *The Titfield Thunderbolt*, a tale of transport rivalry, of English amateurism, spirit and pluck. Titfield is the quintessential village, God-fearing, law-abiding, and full of custom and eccentricity – the sort of place in which the church clock always stands at ten-to-three, where the batsman e'er awaits the bowler and the policeman pounds his beat by bicycle. Faced with losing their branch line – and their way of life – the villagers rally, the villagers propose to run it themselves, and – as they are in a film – they do. Just about.

Whether Elliot saw this Ealing masterpiece is not recorded, but he did know that the real-life closure of loss-making lines and stations was a real-life necessity. In fact, they always had been, the first closure of significance – the Newmarket & Chesterford – coming as early as 1850, when an alternative line (with better connections) was opened by a rival company. The sell-off of hundreds of ex-military lorries after the First World War allowed private hauliers to proliferate and undercut the railway. When coupled with improving vehicle technology and road surfaces, this burgeoning industry – and its bus-based counterpart – began to grow.

Closures dribbled on throughout the 1920s and '30s, but started to increase after nationalisation: in 1951 alone, 133 route miles had been earmarked, while the remnant of the old Stratford-on-Avon & Midland Junction Railway would carry its final passengers the following April. The year after that, BTF shone a light on York and its surroundings, where – out in the dales – defunct branch lines were being replaced by the 'more personal service' offered by bus and van. Track-lifting scenes mingle with those of an intrepid British Railways road vehicle passing 'stations whose level crossing gates have clanged for the last time', en route to pick up parcels in person. It was positive. It was progress. It might not look like that forever ... but at least the cameras showed York itself to be busy; York, where the morning bustle of traders and typists, merchants and clerks is overseen not only by the stationmaster, but also an army of trainspotters, who note every number, survey every service and damp down the dust with lemonade as they pore over their Ian Allan ABCs. Everything works perfectly, every train is on time, every parcel is sorted, every extra carriage added per last-minute plan. The efficiencies on stage are aided behind the scenes by meetings with staff and area officers, who sit round a round table round which concord is king, round which heated debate dissipates and leaves everyone 'breathing agreement all over each other'.

Agreement was also on the breath of Elliot – the former journalist, who'd joined the Southern in 1925, and who tried to get on better with Hurcomb than Missenden had done, despite not being the former's choice to replace the latter on the latter's retirement (a fact Hurcomb told Elliot at their very first meeting). 'If you can help to create a better atmosphere between the Commission and the Executive,' Hurcomb went on, 'we shall be able to get things done'. The trouble was that too often the Commission had trod on the toes of the Executive by trying to manage the railway, instead of shaping policy in the manner it was meant to. Elliot told Hurcomb so, but pleased him by voicing his preference to avoid 'acrimonious correspondence' by meeting more often in person. Yet this ease – if ease it really was – couldn't pull down the iron curtain that persisted between the Commission and the Executive as a whole. And it couldn't make money where there was less and less to be made, for while 1953's gross revenue was up over £18 million on 1952, operating costs had gone up more.

Early BR splendour as ex-LMS 'unrebuilt Scot' No. 46148 *The Manchester Regiment* takes a Carlisle–Glasgow service past Harthope in July 1953 (with a little help from a 2-6-4T at the rear).

An 'intrepid' British Railways Ford Thames ET6 waits to be loaded (or unloaded) at Wenfordbridge goods yard in Cornwall.

'Big Four' experience had shown diesel shunters to be more economical than their steam counterparts. Despite uncertainties about main line diesel traction, the Railway Executive largely agreed. Over 100 locomotives had been delivered by 1953; many more would follow. Here, No. 13240 takes a break at York.

Did you know?

On 24 April 1953, one of Bulleid's Merchant Navy Pacifics – No. 35020 *Bibby Line* – suffered a crank axle failure while passing Crewkerne at around 70 mph. One flying brake block struck a platform support, causing part of it to collapse; another struck a bridge abutment. Thankfully, there were no casualties, though the incident did lead to the temporary withdrawal of the entire class, which led in turn to a number of 'foreign' locomotive types – like ex-LNER Gresley V2s – appearing on Southern metals. It was also partly responsible for the extensive rebuilding programme of the Merchant Navy fleet to a more conventional design. The first 'rebuild' to re-enter traffic would be No. 35018 *British India Line* in 1956 (see page 37); the last would be No. 35028 *Clan Line* four years later. Sixty of the lighter West Country and Battle of Britain Pacifics were also rebuilt between 1957 and 1961.

Unhappy with how the figures starting to fall – and the BTC's over-bureaucratic structure – Churchill's government produced a Transport Act that year which abolished the RE, saw Elliot take over the chair of London Transport and Hurcomb's replacement by General Sir Brian Robertson. Soon the Commission would have direct contact with the regions. Soon the regions would find themselves with new powers. Soon, alas, they would order a phalanx of diesel multiple units tailored to purely local specifications.

Nothing would change; everything would change, for the Act also denationalised the road-haulage industry, launching a sell-off of over 20,000 lorries to private firms, which – like their earlier counterparts – could (and would) undercut the railway – something that increasing numbers of freight customers went on to exploit. So much for the 'efficient, adequate, economical and properly integrated system of public inland transport'. A new solution was needed. A new solution was coming.

But would it be the right one?

Also at York is ex-LNER D20/1 No. 62378, a 4-4-0 design which dated back to 1899. Forty-six D20/1s would be inherited by BR; all would be withdrawn by 1957.

In many ways the Somerset & Dorset line, which connected Bath to Bournemouth via the Mendip hills, was the epitome of the steam railway. Here, a trio of former Midland engines waits at Bath Green Park shed.

4
Modernisation ... Strikes

Today you are one of the hundreds. One of the hundreds on 'The Elizabethan' at King's Cross. The morning is June. The weather is fine. The time for departure is half-past nine. You take your place in an elegant coach, having battled through bustle, trilby hats, Windsmoor coats ... to watch supplies handed up from platform to train, and the guard as he checks on his watch yet again. Parcels pass by on barrow and trolley, as a late-comer boards on her way to see Molly. Or was it Jean? Or June? Or dear old Aunt Dolly?

Your musing done, a whistle comes, and the train starts with a jolt so genteel. You light a cigar, head to the bar, and smile at the irony you feel.

Irony? Yes, for you are living out (almost *exactly*, it seems) BTF's rhyming new short, *Elizabethan Express*. But of course that film – that celebration of steam, of travel, of travel by rail – isn't just about you, isn't just about 'the Howards, the Berts, the Cynthias, the Mabels' – it's about the driver taking control of his charge, the fireman creating a fine head of steam, the signalman keeping the traffic moving safely, the platelayer keeping the track in good order, the train planner creating a smooth-running timetable, the waiters waiting, the upholsterers upholstering, the fitters fitting... and of course the locomotive itself – Gresley's mighty A4. These elegant engines – born in the Art Deco era of the thirties – were now powering passengers from King's Cross to Edinburgh in just 6½ hours, an achievement partly inspired by the accession of Princess Elizabeth to the throne in 1953, partly allowed by permanent way improvements that let trains be run at higher, 'pre-war' speeds.

It seemed like there was something for passengers to be happy about at last, though in reality the world of traditions and timetables, of stationmasters in top hats and spanner-wielding artisans was not all it seemed, the trouble being that rising standards of living were driving more people towards the products of Morris, Ford, Austin and the apparent freedom they brought. This – coupled with increasing operating costs, lagging fares, lagging charges and the loss of freight to road – began to turn BR's surplus into a deficit.

'The Elizabethan' was a non-stop King's Cross–Edinburgh Waverley express that ran between 1953 and 1962. Power was usually provided by an ex-LNER A4, as this contemporary postcard demonstrates.

At Carlisle Kingmoor depot, 'Royal Scot' No. 46140 *The King's Royal Rifle Corps* takes over the 'Royal Scot' from Coronation Pacific No. 46222 *Queen Mary*.

Did you know?

It wasn't just the 'Elizabethan' that had speeded up by 1954 – 'The Bristolian' was allowing City businessmen to reach Bristol in 105 minutes, just like they had before the war, the 'Royal Scot' between Euston and Glasgow had 30 minutes shaved off its time, while the two-hour schedule between Paddington and Birmingham Snow Hill also reappeared.

The hard work over, King class No. 6015 *King Richard III* sits 'on the blocks' at Paddington, having just completed the high-speed dash up from Bristol with 'The Bristolian' in 1954.

BR's problems weren't only about money, of course: they were also about men, and with Britain now enjoying full employment (or something very like it), men like the ones recognised in *Elizabethan Express* were getting harder to find, as fewer and fewer of them wanted to get covered in soot and grime cleaning, firing and maintaining locomotives – despite what some of them might have thought as boys. Steam locomotives demanded a lot of looking after and could take up to two hours to prepare for traffic, even after the boiler had been filled and the fire lit. True, they were built from indigenous materials and powered by indigenous fuel, but recent coal shortages, price rises and concerns about quality had weakened this benefit considerably. Add in growing concerns about pollution and the parlous state of BR's finances, and it was clear that drastic measures were needed if the company was to remain competitive. And, in 1954, 'drastic measures' meant the death of the old, the shock of the new, and something that seemed like it could solve the asset problems, the financial problems and the staffing problems in one fell swoop. A modernisation committee was duly established, and published its findings at the end of that year.

The plan behind *The Modernisation and Re-Equipment of British Railways* was supported by the government, which set aside £1,200 million of public money to be spent on it over fifteen years. The aim was to 'exploit the great natural advantages of railways as bulk transporters of passengers and goods and to revolutionise the character of the services provided for both'. With Riddles having retired, and technology having moved on, this 'revolution' would not only involve mechanisation, more colour-light signalling, and even more permanent way improvements, it'd also involve the substitution of steam by diesel as well as electric traction. The Plan noted that much 'useful experience' had been gained with the designs BR had inherited, and asserted that 'in view of the high degree of reliability attained in other countries where diesel traction has been widely adopted, there is no reason to doubt that equally satisfactory results will be realised here'.

In March 1954, No. 10203 – the 2,000 hp variant of the diesel locomotive design Bulleid produced for the Southern Railway – emerged from Brighton Works. It is seen at Exeter Central that July.

In 1951, the Railway Executive appointed a Committee to assess the feasibility of using lightweight diesel multiple units on branches and cross-country routes. The first trains began to appear in 1954. This view shows a Park Royal example at Boston the following year.

It was an optimistic view, many of those designs having fallen decidedly short of expectations, a lack of spares often combining with a lack of know-how (though it didn't help that repairs were often made under 'steam conditions', whose dirt and grime were hardly conducive to the fine tolerances needed to keep a diesel engine in fine fettle). When working properly, those on BR's books could put in some good performances, it was true, but their overall record was somewhat erratic and saw many long periods out of service.

Did you know?

Born in India in July 1896, Brian Robertson was educated at Charterhouse and the Royal Military Academy, Woolwich, before serving with the Royal Engineers in France and Italy during the First World War (where he was mentioned in despatches). He later joined the War Office in Military Intelligence, resigning his commission in 1935 to become managing director of Dunlop.

Having re-joined the Army in 1940, he went on to be Commander-in-Chief of the Middle East Land Forces and Governor of the Suez Canal Zone. He retired from the Army for a second time in 1953 to take up the chairmanship of the BTC. Though a stickler for discipline, as one might expect, he was also at ease with front line staff and was well respected by them.

Robertson tried to reorganise the BTC by creating a three-tier system of management, complete with a military-style 'General Staff' – a move that proved unpopular with career managers. He also supported the 'Modernisation Plan', which he saw as a way of stemming the flow of cash away from the industry.

After retirement in 1961, he was created Baron Robertson of Oakridge. He died in April 1974, aged seventy-seven.

Still, like many things from the minds of managers, modernisation looked good on paper, and a 'Pilot Scheme' was duly developed to test various power levels, wheel arrangements and transmission systems. Speaking at a press conference, Robertson acknowledged that BR's problems had been exacerbated by old and obsolete equipment, yet he knew too that,

In December 1953, the first EM2 class electric emerged to work expresses on the 1,500 V DC electrified line between Manchester and Sheffield – the so-called 'Woodhead' route. Here, No. 27001 is seen at Woodhead itself, entering the new tunnel at that location, which opened in June 1954.

while improving this situation would 'produce its own economies', new equipment – of any kind – was 'not the only necessary ingredient for good railways'. He hoped the Plan would put 'heart into the whole industry, and convince all who work in it that they belong to a live show with a fine future, and not to a decaying anachronism'.

Sadly, he reckoned without the Associated Society of Locomotive Engineers and Firemen – ASLEF – who went on strike over pay and conditions from midnight on 28 May. By 1 June – on the advice of ministers – the Queen was declaring a state of emergency. Soon, postal services would be disrupted. Soon Trooping the Colour would have to be cancelled. It was an outrage! It was a disgrace! It was all getting a bit much … though you probably didn't have much if you were actually on the strike, on the picket line, waiting, pocket emptying, food dwindling, as one week became two and started looking like three.

Seventeen days it lasted; seventeen days later the men were back at work while Lord Justice Morris considered their claim. The first major railway stoppage for thirty years had cost the Commission some £12 million, but there was another price to pay. 'Coal and steel are our life's blood, and the railways are the arteries along which they must flow,' said Pathé News, but though iron, steel, coal (and therefore the electricity supply) were seriously affected – as were London commuters – it was clear that a national rail strike was no longer going to paralyse the nation. With most National Union of Railwaymen members still driving trains, pulling signal levers and checking tickets, BR managed to carry a quarter of its passenger traffic and a third of its freight, although many of the freight customers who switched to road for the duration would never come back, it had to be said.

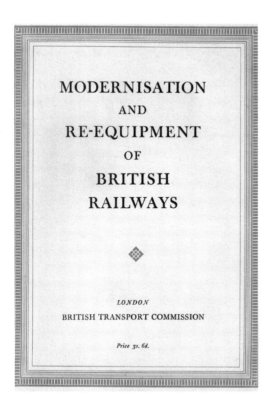

Above left: The 'Modernisation Plan', which was published at the very end of 1954, and which would bring such great change to Britain's railways.

Above right: By 1955, there were over 3 million cars on Britain's roads; the first section of motorway would open just three years later. This contemporary poster tries to help redress the balance, but though BR's fears about road competition would be well-founded, passenger receipts still rose by £2 million in 1959.

Right: Some of the 'holiday returns' advertised by this brochure would have been disrupted by the 1955 strike, which ran for seventeen days from midnight on 28 May.

General Sir Brian Robertson, Chairman of the British Transport Commission, 1953–61, seen talking to staff at Newton Abbot depot in 1954.

By the time orders for 174 diesel locomotives had been placed with a number of manufacturers that November, the public – if not the unionists – had largely forgotten the strike and the newsreels were reeling to the sight of a vision in powder blue. Not part of the Modernisation Plan, this was a private speculation that came about when D. Napier & Sons – an English Electric subsidiary – produced a lightweight, high-powered engine for Royal Navy patrol vessels, and the parent company used a pair to test their suitability for railway applications. The result – *Deltic* – was the most powerful locomotive in the world when it appeared the following year.

With half an eye on the export market, the styling, with its cream aluminium bodyside beading and curved chevrons, was reminiscent of American practice, a trait captured best by the large headlight housing fitted to each nose end (although the lights themselves were never installed). Some loved it, others hated it, but when trials began on the London Midland Region most commentators concentrated on performance. At first, EE asked that the locomotive be kept off passenger turns, lest the complexity of the 3,300 hp design – and the unreliability of its steam heating boilers – led to reputation-damaging repairs in service. Allocated to Liverpool's Edge Hill depot, it started work on 13 December, finishing 1955 on overnight freights to and from the capital. In time, its success would see it take charge of the 'Merseyside Express'. In time, it would impress the Eastern with the power – and timetable opportunities – it seemed to offer. In time, the production versions would take over from Gresley's A4, a new roar usurping its 'speed of a greyhound, strength of a boar'. It was progress. But there was always a price to be paid. By someone.

Deltic working the Up 'Merseyside Express' past Halton Junction. The name derived from the locomotive's triangular cylinder arrangement, but the styling was reminiscent of American practice, reflecting the fact that English Electric hoped for a flood of export orders. Sadly, they never came and *Deltic* was donated to the Science Museum in 1963.

5
Rebuilds and New Builds

It's just after half two and a freight pulls in to the yard to drop a couple off, pick a couple up. Couplings clang and whistles sound as the driver and fireman chat away to their relief. Walking along the ballast, the new guard greets the old and – pleasantries exchanged, wagons rearranged – checks the tail lamp while the wheeltapper plies his trade. The sound of cold metal on cold rings true (thank goodness), as the guard glances at the paperwork. The train's unfitted from top to tail – it was going to be a slow old run. He heads to his van and winds the handbrake on to make sure it's working. It is. All is well. He stows his gear, checks the stove and shines his lamp towards the cab. When 'the off' comes, he settles so he can keep an eye on things from the ducket window. He always does this for unfitted freights; unfitted freights can be troublesome – especially when there's a descent to be made ...

... and soon – soonish, after being looped and let out, looped and let out – that descent comes. They pull in again, but this time the train slows while the guard climbs down to insert a 'cricket bat' stick in every other underframe to force down the handbrakes. It's a dangerous job, though less dangerous than the train running away should a coupling break or the driver lose control...

In 1955, there were around 1,000 locations where the handbrakes had to be pinned down like this. But what had to be pinned down also had to be 'unpinned' at some point – and it was costing BR around 10,000 man hours a week. Thankfully, the Modernisation Plan was set to put a stop to all those 'Emett-like trains' that went 'clankety-clank through our countryside' (as Robertson described them) by urging the wider adoption of continuous vacuum brakes. Not only would this get rid of the pinning problem, but also the need for catch points on gradients more severe than 1 in 260. It would allow freight train speeds to be increased to

At Gloucester Eastgate, Standard class 5 No. 73065 has the road, while Patriot No. 45519 *Lady Godiva* takes on water and 4F 0-6-0 No. 44272 waits to head south with a freight.

36

Above: The goods would get there, but progress could be slow, as 'pick-up' services fed into marshalling yards, where wagons would be shunted into longer trains for long-distance transit. More marshalling and unloading would ensue before final delivery. At Glenfield, the shunter considers the next move, while ex-Midland 3F No. 58247 simmers in the platform.
Below: Newly rebuilt Merchant Navy Pacific No. 35018 *British India Line* awaits its next turn of duty soon after conversion.

something closer to those for passenger trains too, which would in turn increase capacity on the main line, improve punctuality and 'lead to a reduction of about 2,000 in the number of locomotives, with a saving in interest, depreciation and maintenance costs'.

Among those capable of these higher speeds was the final Riddles design – the 9F 2-10-0s – which were still emerging from Swindon and Crewe. With a tractive effort approaching 40,000 lb, they were soon dubbed 'spaceships' by trainspotters awed by their size and shape. They would go on to put in some impressive performances, surprising some railwaymen into believing they must have lost half their train, such was the ease with which they could take inclines that would leave lesser engines needing another one to assist. By this time, though, Riddles' main line ideal – electrification – was also starting to gain pace.

Allowing intensive services to be operated by combining low running costs with high acceleration, electrification was especially attractive for concentrated commuter lines, as the Southern Railway had found when it completed its conversion of the London suburban network in 1929. The LMS and LNER also inherited and developed various schemes, although the latter's Liverpool Street–Shenfield route was energised under BR in 1949. Its scheme to raise the wires on the 'Woodhead' between Manchester, Sheffield and Wath – stymied first by economic crisis, then by the outbreak of war – had finally come to fruition in 1955.

Both the Shenfield and Woodhead lines featured direct current (DC) supply systems. The Southern had favoured a 750 volt direct current passed through a third rail to the train's traction motors via 'shoes' attached to the bogies. The Woodhead was also powered by DC, but at twice the voltage via overhead line equipment (OLE). Riddles, however, had been impressed by French railway experience with an alternating current (AC). Indeed, one of his final acts as a railwayman had been to initiate trials of fifty-cycle AC traction between Lancaster, Morecambe and Heysham. This was the future and BR's 'Development Programme'

Of the twelve 'Standard' classes, arguably the most successful was the 9F 2-10-0, introduced in January 1954 for fast and heavy freights. Here, No. 92002 stands outside Swindon Works that February. Some 9Fs also worked passenger services, notably on the Somerset & Dorset line.

MODERNISATION
OF BRITISH RAILWAYS

THE SYSTEM

OF

ELECTRIFICATION.

FOR

BRITISH

RAILWAYS

◆

BRITISH
TRANSPORT COMMISSION
LONDON

Right: *The System of Electrification for British Railways* – an addendum to the 'Modernisation Plan' – was published in 1956. It showed that 'switching on' Euston–Manchester–Liverpool with an AC current would cost £117.8 million, against £123.6 million for doing so with DC.
Below: On 31 October 1956, the last steam engine to be built to a pre-nationalisation design – Pannier tank No .3409 – entered service in Cardiff.

of April 1953 had explained how £160 million would be spent on electrifying from King's Cross to Newcastle, Euston to Birmingham, Manchester, Liverpool and Glasgow, St Pancras to Manchester, and Paddington to Bristol and South Wales. Soon derailed by that year's Transport Act, alas, it would be 1956 before the comparative costs would be known.

Did you know?

The Western's absence from *The System of Electrification for British Railways* underlined that it had failed to meet the necessary financial criteria for conversion. However, the region's Area Board decided it wanted to be able to assess the situation for itself. The BTC was subsequently approached and Messrs Merz & McLellan were duly appointed to embark on a 'fair and economic' appraisal of the Paddington–Cardiff routes via Bristol Temple Meads and Badminton 'to indicate the probable outlay involved [...] and to furnish a comparison of the cost of operation with that of diesel traction'. A pilot study was in progress by October 1957, the findings being published in May 1959.

That the figures were not attractive enough would eventually lead the Western down a quite different path (see page 50).

In fact, *The System of Electrification for British Railways* showed that 'switching on' Euston–Manchester–Liverpool with AC would save almost £6 million against doing so with DC, an economy that centred on the size of the contact wire and OLE, the number of substations required, the power distribution arrangements, and the clearances that would have to be provided for bridges and tunnels. AC traction also enjoyed better adhesion, which allowed the use of lighter, more amenable locomotives that didn't waste power in the main resistances for speed control, and which could also supply electricity for train heating and lighting more cheaply and conveniently. 'Taking an overall view,' the report when on, 'the Commission are satisfied that the AC system offers substantial economies both in first costs and in annual costs of operation. They consider that the system will permit of the electrification in the future of certain secondary lines whose electrification by the DC system could not be financially justified.'

By the end of the decade, BR would be gearing up for the start of electric services between Crewe and Manchester... But the end of the decade was still four years away, that year's distance from the bright new world perhaps shown best by the fact it saw the first rebuilt Merchant Navy and the last locomotive built to a pre-nationalisation design accepted to traffic. It was also the first year receipts failed to cover expenses. On the surface, it would seem that salvation – in traction terms, at least – was going to come from Riddles' least-favoured option...

Fast-forward to 3 June 1957, and a gleaming green beast waits while a man makes a speech. Soon, another man will turn a handle and the locomotive will burst into life as light trips off its bufferbeam... We're watching D8000, the first so-called 'Pilot Scheme' prototype to be completed. We're watching with the crowd at the Vulcan Foundry, Newton-le-Willows, marvelling at the fact that – in fifteen days' time – the machine we've worked on will be delivered to BR.

Between 1958 and 1960, twenty-four electric locomotives were built at BR's Doncaster Works for the newly electrified Kent Coast Main Line. Soon to be found working boat trains like the 'Golden Arrow' and 'Night Ferry', E5004 is seen at Eastleigh in 1959.

Our employer – English Electric – had been behind *Deltic* and the power units in Nos 10000, 10001 and 10201–3, was no stranger to the export and domestic industrial markets, and was unique in being the only British company able to manufacture a diesel locomotive's mechanical parts, engine and electric transmission. Yet these were still uncharted waters for its customer, BR having already reneged on its Modernisation Plan pledge to assess the Pilot Scheme properly, ordering a further 143 locomotives before the first had turned a wheel, as it clamoured to cut costs, beat recruitment problems and comply with the Clean Air Act of 1956.

Did you know?

On the foggy evening of 4 December 1957, a train for Hayes pulled up at a red signal at Parks Bridge Junction, Lewisham. The fog was causing delays, leading some trains to be out of their timetabled order. The signalman wanted to confirm the train's destination and identity. At 6:20 p.m., a train from Cannon Street passed a signal at danger and struck the Hayes service in rear. The impact threw the tender and leading coach of the second train into a column supporting a bridge carrying the Nunhead–Lewisham line. The bridge subsided on to the train below, completing the destruction of the leading coach, crushing the second and the front half of the third. In all, ninety people were killed and 176 were injured.

D8000 fell into the Type 1 power category, able to exert 42,000 lb of tractive effort via its 1,000 hp engine. Based on a design built for New Zealand and Tasmania, all twenty of the first batch were allocated to the new diesel depot at Devons Road, Bow. From here, they were put to work on cross-London freights, their characteristic chirruping exhausts soon echoing

Above: English Electric Type 1 D8000 is seen on test at Frodsham in May 1957, soon before delivery to BR. In all, 228 locomotives of this design would be built, production resuming after its superiority over the proposed 'standard' for the 800–1,000 hp power range (the Clayton Type 1 – see *The Sixties Railway*) had become all too apparent.

Below: The D8200s were designed by British Thomson-Houston and built between 1957 and 1961. D8220 is seen at Ipswich in original livery.

BR inherited a number of ships from the Big Four and continued to operate ferry services to the Channel Islands, Isle of Wight and France, among others. This timetable for 1957 provides details of the steamer services that BR provided between Heysham and Belfast.

NORTHERN IRELAND
VIA
HEYSHAM
BELFAST

STEAMER SERVICES

17th June to 15th September 1957

BRITISH RAILWAYS

SEE SEPARATE FOLDER FOR DETAILS OF SAILINGS ON WHICH SAILING TICKETS ARE REQUIRED

round the upper reaches of Willesden Junction, where Ivatt Class 4s had once reigned supreme. Performances were impressive and they soon outpaced their fellow Type 1s, the British Thomson-Houston D8200s and North British-built D8400s, both of whose Paxman engines used sixteen cylinders for a mere 800 hp, against the eight of the more powerful English Electric machine. More cylinders meant high maintenance costs for low power from an engine whose cylinder heads were prone to cracking, whose pistons were prone to seizure, and whose engine rooms were not unknown to fire.

But 1,000 hp wasn't enough for all the lower-grade work BR believed it had and – of the five contenders in the 1,000–1,500 hp Type 2 category – the first to appear would be D5500, a mixed traffic unit built by Brush Traction of Loughborough. Like EE, Brush had experience of the export market, having secured an order for twenty-five locomotives for the Ceylon Government Railway in 1950. Completed in September 1957, D5500 was tested before being allocated to Stratford depot on 31 October – an appropriate day in the eyes of many local railwaymen, who watched this 'demon' arrive with some suspicion, sensing that their working lives were about to change. They were right, of course, though at first the revolt came not with a roar, but a whimper, the locomotive and its nineteen classmates seemingly underpowered for the semi-fast passenger duties the Operating Department had in mind for them. There were also problems with their control gear and, consequently, many failures. As a result, the D5000 series – built to BR's own design, using Sulzer engines and British Thomson-Houston electrical equipment – would go on to be the 'standard' Type 2. Eventually. In the meantime, while decisions were being made, minds changed and arguments lost, somewhere in a Norfolk rectory a vicar was writing a satire of the whole situation. 'We are revolutionary,' one character would claim of his kind. A litany of lies and errors would put a stamp on steam's superiority. A litany of lies and errors would see the deceitful incomer sent packing. But by the time the Reverend Awdry's *Duck and the Diesel Engine* had been published, the tide of new traction was growing too strong and the changes they brought too much to resist...

D8404 is seen in pristine condition at Stratford. Like the D8200s, the D8400s suffered piston and cylinder head problems soon after their introduction.

Only the outermost axles on the three-axle bogies beneath the D5500s were powered, giving them an 'A1A-A1A' wheel arrangement, the 'A' denoting the powered axles, the '1' denoting the unpowered ones. Here, D5515 has its steam heating boiler topped up at King's Lynn.

Originally seen as the 'standard' Type 2 design, the D5000s would start to appear in 1958. In this view, D5000 itself hauls a fifteen-coach test train over Newtown Viaduct that September.

6
Gaining Traction

You're fourteen years old, soon to be fifteen, soon to leave school. You've always loved railways, but now it's time to start thinking about a job, you just aren't sure. Then, one Saturday, the answer comes to you. There you are, sitting in the fusty fug of your local Odeon, waiting for Roy Rogers or Will Hay, when the lights flicker and instead you see *A Future on Rail*, a recruitment short made by British Transport Films. You'd seen *Elizabethan Express* – you'd seen *The Titfield Thunderbolt* – but this is different: this is offering a window of opportunity on a changing world. Not that it was going to be right for everyone – those Stratford drivers and their ilk are shown through the eyes of one such 'climbing into a diesel as if it was the grave'.

And to many men, it *was* the grave. To many men, it was the end of the life they knew – the life of dignity, of heroism, even. Mind you, not everyone felt that way. In the film, 'these drivers' soon learn to enjoy the comforts of the cab after the toil and heat and sweat of the footplate. And diesels certainly were cleaner than steam. They also required less maintenance and were ready for action at the touch of a button – or they were when they worked. Fires, flashovers and failures were not uncommon among some, while the sudden influx of new traction types could give drivers four, five or six different diesel classes with which to familiarise themselves. Depots too felt the strain as the training programme cut the number of crews available to work their normal services and the number of artisans on shed to keep things running.

Old and new side by side in 1958, as a Swindon-built diesel multiple unit approaches Cheltenham, while ex-GWR No.4966 *Shakenhurst Hall* plods along with a two-coach 'local'.

A glimpse into the future in the form of the newly opened Margam Marshalling Yard. Note the retarders after the second set of points, and the control tower top left.

Depots of another kind were changing too, and the film made no bones about it, BR now replacing many old-fashioned goods yards with a smaller number of mechanised ones, where palletised goods were shifted by fork-lift trucks, cranes and conveyor belts instead of armies of muscle-bound men. And then there were the marshalling yards, about which plenty was afoot: the Eastern Region was working on a new one at Temple Mills; the London Midland was preparing a scheme for Swanbourne; the Southern was considering new yards at Eastleigh and Tonbridge; while the Western was completing plans for Margam. The Scottish Region's yard at Thornton had opened at the end of 1956, and was the first in Britain to incorporate automated primary and secondary retarders, designed to slow wagons free-wheeling down a man-made hump. As with anything new and complicated, there were teething problems, but by 1957 Thornton was sorting up to 2,000 wagons every day.

Shame freight was in such decline. Shame that many of these yards would end up as wagonload 'white elephants', whose fully fitted trains brought decreasing amounts of produce across the green tablecloth of the country. Shame... Still, *A Future on Rail* had no business dealing with that side of things and the film ends with a schoolboy looking excitedly past the driver and through the windscreen of a diesel multiple unit. The latter were starting to provide improved services on an increasing number of lines, though if anything about the modern(ising) railway was going to excite the younger element, it was more likely going to be one of the throbbing diesel locomotives, deliveries of which continued throughout 1958, the D5000s being joined by the Crossley-engined D5700s from July, the BRCW-built D5300s from August and the North British D6100s at the end of the year. The D5300s were the most successful, being tested largely on the Eastern before settling down for a short spell on the Great Northern, ahead of their migration to Scotland early in the next decade.

Did you know?

The D5700s were noted for their unusual wheel arrangement, having one two-axle bogie and one three-axle bogie, but what really set them apart was their use of a two-stroke engine, Crossley's version having enjoyed good reports from the Admiralty. This – plus the fact that Oliver Bulleid was trying the same arrangement in Ireland using Metrovick electrical equipment – led to a Pilot Scheme order for twenty.

Maybe it was because Navy use would have been at a generally constant loading, whereas rail applications involve a constant cycling of power to meet the varying requirements of a journey; maybe it was the Navy's use of on-board engineers for running repairs. Either way, Crossley's good name soon began to drown in a sea of engine failures. One of the worst problems involved stress cracking on the crankcase, which led (*inter alia*) to a programme of major works – and a decision not to re-order.

'Metrovick' D5702 heads east away from Disley Tunnel with a Manchester–Derby service.

Diesels would also be put to use on some of the new named trains introduced in 1958, there having been a realisation that early morning business services were somewhat absent from the timetable. Thus, the London Midland launched 'The Caledonian', which set off from Euston at 7:45 a.m. and – after stopping at Crewe and Carlisle – reached Glasgow Central at half two. September also saw the birth of the 'Master Cutler' – a diesel-hauled Pullman service that reached Sheffield from the capital in 2 hours 45 minutes. Faster trains like these

Having crossed over the Forth Bridge, BRCW Type 2s D5310 and D5311 take a passenger train through Dalmeny station.

meant more powerful locomotives, preferably of 2,000 hp or more. In the case of the 'Master Cutler', that power would come from English Electric, whose 'Type 4' was a development of No. 10203. Like No. 10203, it was a heavyweight machine, which also required four axles per bogie to spread the load and allow it to run over routes engineered to lighter standards. The doyen, D200, had been delivered to the Eastern Region in March. For a short time, it and the remaining nine of the order became 'top link' machines. Yet Robertson was unimpressed, believing the class incapable of maintaining high speeds when hauling heavy trains.

His theory was proved correct when the loading was anything above seven coaches, flashovers being frequent when running fast, although their bulk was a boon when working (or rather, trying to stop) long unfitted freights. Solid enough for BR to order a further 190, they failed to replace steam on East Coast Main Line expresses, although they did become a regular feature on the London Midland, where they tackled the steep Camden Bank north of Euston with ease, and where the need for long periods of sustained speed was less acute.

The other Pilot Scheme Type 4 was built by BR's own Derby Works. The LM's Mechanical Engineering Department was more interested in the Sulzer engine, yet the resulting locomotives (D1–10) were just as heavy as their EE counterparts and therefore just as ill-suited to high-speed passenger work. Reallocation was one solution to the 'weight problem', but another was found on the Continent, where the German State Railway's lightweight diesel-hydraulic locomotives had been acquitting themselves admirably. Riddles' successor, R. C. Bond, had expressed an interest in testing locomotives of this type after witnessing trials of two units North British had built for Mauritius. As the company had also prepared designs for 1,000 and 2,000 hp machines suitable for the home market, Bond pressed the

Above: Despite a poor reputation for unreliability, there would eventually be fifty-eight NBL diesel-electric Type 2s on BR's books. By the end of 1960, all would be allocated to the Scottish Region – allegedly to bring them closer to their Glasgow-based manufacturer for repairs under warranty! Here, brand-new D6112 is seen at Doncaster Works.
Below: A postcard showing an English Electric Type 4 working 'The Flying Scotsman'.

10494 "The Flying Scotsman" hauled by
Class 4 Diesel Electric Locomotive. British Railways Photo.

Commission to add both to the Pilot Scheme, so they could be assessed against diesel-electric traction. Though the Chief Electrical Engineer was unimpressed, orders were duly placed for eleven locomotives in February 1955.

It made sense to concentrate the 'hydraulics' in one area and, in this, Bond had the full support of the Western Region, which looked favourably on the concept, partly because of its limited experience of electrics, and partly because there were no plans to electrify the lines out of Paddington (meaning it was faced not so much with a longer-term dieselisation programme than intended for the other regions, but a *complete* one). There was a chance that a hydraulic strategy would help it make the best of this situation. And there were certain benefits.

For one thing, the German V200 series featured aircraft-style stressed-skin ('monocoque') construction, which allowed them to combine high power and low weight – a configuration that could increase haulage capacity by two coaches. And any concerns that a lighter locomotive would be less suitable for heavy freight were allayed by the Modernisation Plan pledge that loose-coupled goods trains were to be abolished.

The first diesel-hydraulic to emerge from North British was D600, a Type 4. Officially completed in November 1957, it enjoyed a good press run between Paddington and Bristol Temple Meads on 17 February 1958, though one of its twin engines cut out soon after departing with the return working. But while the locomotive and its classmates put up some good performances in their first two years, it could be argued that they failed to exploit the full potential of the diesel-hydraulic, being – at 117.5 tons – not so very different from their diesel-electric competitors, and certainly not comparable to the V200s (on which the WR looked as the 'ideal'). Thankfully, German manufacturer Maybach had offered the Region a set of powertrains in March 1955, thus giving Swindon the chance to construct a scaled-down version.

The BTC approved an order for three of these locomotives the following February, the first of which – D800 – emerged from Swindon Works in June 1958, some 29 tons lighter than its North British counterpart. After being named *Sir Brian Robertson* the following month it was put to work on the famous

A leaflet produced by British Railways to promote its modernisation programme for 1957/8. Its proud claim is that the programme would ensure services would 'go on improving until they are the finest and most modern in the world'.

Above: Not all named trains fell immediately to the new diesels. In this 1958 view, Bulleid West Country No. 34092 *City of Wells* prepares to come off Stewarts Lane depot to work the celebrated 'Golden Arrow'.

Below: One of the original batch of North British-built diesel-hydraulics – D601, later to be named *Ark Royal* – awaits acceptance trials at Swindon's new diesel shed in March 1958.

Above: Swindon-built D800 class diesel-hydraulic D801 *Vanguard* awaits the 'Right Away' at Westbury. Like the D600s, almost all D800s were named after British warships – hence the 'Warship' nickname. The bogie problem suffered by this class (mentioned in the text) had been solved by 1963.

Below: The old railway continued to tempt the enthusiast, as shown by the crowds at Barmouth in 1958. The locomotive coupled to the coaches is No. 9017, a member of the so-called 'Dukedog' class, which was built at Swindon in 1938, using frames from Bulldog No. 3425 (built 1906), and boiler and cab from Duke No. 3282 (built 1899). It would later be preserved.

In December 1958, BR began experimenting with four-wheeled diesel railbuses in a bid to save operating costs and encourage patronage on its minor branches. In this view, Park Royal machine M79973 awaits a turn at Bedford.

'Cornish Riviera Express' from Paddington to Plymouth. Despite poor riding on pointwork or poorly maintained track, thanks to the way the bogies were attached, performances were impressive and 100 mph was often exceeded. As a result, no further D600s were ordered, though there would eventually be thirty-eight 'Swindon' Type 4s and thirty-three similar locomotives built by North British, which was also responsible for the D6300 series Type 2s that entered traffic from January 1959. Sadly, this lower-powered design soon started to suffer engine and transmission faults, such that – before long – there would be delays, there would be failures, there would be locos laid up in sidings. Before long, there would also be change. Again.

7
Cometh the Hour?

It can't have been easy being Sir Brian. Running the railways – running any sort of transport organisation – was something of a thankless task. It was probably worse after they became publicly owned. At least before – under the Big Four – there were only shareholders to answer to; now there was the Minister, the Ministry, the press, Pathé, the people ... the men ... all wanting to know what was happening to 'their money'.

Ex-LMS Class 4 No. 43108 leaves Yarmouth Beach with a train for South Lynn. Both stations were on the Midland & Great Northern route, which was closed in 1959, as described in the text.

Did you know?

By 1959, deliveries of diesel multiple units had reached about 80 per cent of the planned total of 4,000. The first of the new trains were deployed in the West Riding of Yorkshire and West Cumberland, but they soon made their presence felt across the regions. Fairly reliable (once their maintenance regimes had been ironed out), they 'completely changed the picture of travel by rail' on some routes, according to the BTC at least. Yet, while some services – like those between Sheffield and Barnsley – saw revenue triple, others – like those between Aberdeen and Peterhead – saw an increase of less than a tenth. It was admitted that some of the routes converted from steam had never been expected to show 'first class' results, and that many to which the public failed to respond would have to be withdrawn.

A Derby two-car unit waits at Norwich City after arriving from Melton Constable.

Robertson would later tell his predecessor that when he accepted Churchill's invitation 'to command one hundred thousand men', he didn't know the management had been 'destroyed' before he got there. In the valley of death left by the Railway Executive's abolition, he set about creating a military style 'General Staff', which he thought would aid efficiency. Alas it was unpopular – and expensive – though not as expensive perhaps as the Modernisation Plan, for which 1959 was going to be something of a turning point…

D5718 on the 'Condor' – BR's Anglo-Scottish express freight service, which was launched in June 1959. Alas, the D5700s proved so unreliable on this train that customer demand dropped until alternative traction was provided.

On the one hand, it was to be celebrated. Robertson certainly believed in it, and BTF provided a twenty-minute colour report on all its achievements so far, achievements that included improvements to track, to locomotives and rolling stock, staff training, stations, marshalling yards and depots. On the other hand, it also included electrification. And electrification was expensive. Very expensive. Whitehall was starting to make uncomfortable noises about costs and deficits and cuts. With pressure mounting to reassess the Plan, the Commission bit the bullet and produced a 'reappraisal', which appeared at the end of July.

It was, it said, 'a complete review' in the light of 'economic and technical developments which have occurred since its conception and of future economic and technical trends'. It was, in fact, honest about the rising costs, which were due in part to 'all-round increases in prices', but also 'to the more precise evaluation of certain parts of the Plan'. Well, the first lot of rising costs were. The second lot were down to a need 'to get the best results from continuous braking' (meaning 'certain further expenditure on equipment for freight vehicles'), the need 'to maintain the new types of motive power and rolling stock at their maximum efficiency' (meaning 'developments at depots which were not contemplated at the time of the preparation of the Plan') and the need for 'some further works necessary at passenger stations'. The 'reappraisal' also insisted the Modernisation Plan was soundly based, and must be 'pressed forward at a rate faster [...] than planned hitherto', in order to speed 'the improvements on which future revenues depend'.

This saw even more orders placed for largely untested locomotives – which is why, despite the railway's resolve to eliminate all the under-performing North British Type 2 diesel-electrics, it still ended up with fifty-eight of them.

If that sounds pricey, it was, and though passenger receipts rose by £2 million and operating costs fell in 1959, BR's deficit was mounting. The company had been trying to save money by expanding its fleet of multiple units and railbuses, and by closing loss-making lines. Indeed, February had seen the closure of an entire route – the Midland & Great Northern from Peterborough to Great Yarmouth. This, the 'Muddle and Go Nowhere', had never prospered, attracting mainly local agricultural and horticultural traffic. Complete closure had been mooted the year before and had been approved by the Transport Users Consultative Committee within a couple of months. It was thought at least £640,000 could be saved per annum, but it was a drop in the ocean created by raising the wires between London and Liverpool. Still, at least the locomotive side of electrification was proving less wasteful than the Pilot Scheme...

The first 25 kV machine had started life as No. 18100 – the second of two gas turbine locomotives the Great Western had ordered before nationalisation. It'd emerged from Metropolitan Vickers in October 1958, re-motored and renumbered, and started driver training turns on the Styal line. It was soon joined by five 'test' classes, which – like their diesel counterparts – were produced by a number of builders, including BR itself. This time, though, BR imposed certain requirements, like the basic body shape, axle load, weight and wheel arrangement. It also wanted each type to be able to take a 475-ton passenger train from Manchester to London at a maximum speed of 100 mph and a 950-ton freight over the same route at an average speed of 42.

The first of the new breed to emerge was E3001, an 'AL1' which had been built by the Birmingham Carriage & Wagon Company and officially handed over to BR at a press reception at Sandbach in November. It was the shape of things to come, a herald for a new railway age. Perhaps. Some felt the Modernisation Plan and its 'reappraisal' were just too far from reality. The government – newly emboldened by an increased majority gained in that year's General Election – shared that view. It would not be long before Prime Minister Harold Macmillan, a former director of the GWR, put his faith in Ernest Marples, a road-engineering contractor involved in motorway construction. To avoid any conflict of interest, the new transport minister would divest himself of his shares in the Marples, Ridgeway company – to his wife, as it turned out. In the years ahead, he would be accused of impropriety and much more. In the months ahead, he would appoint a special committee to find ways of upping efficiency and cutting costs.

Imagine, then, being a railway officer a few days from Christmas 1959. You're at Paddington, it's cold, and as you sip a coffee in the warmth of the restaurant, you look out at the platforms and the milling millions. It's still a cathedral of steam, but modernisation is making its presence

The changing face of London's Liverpool Street in July 1959, as a Traction Inspector poses alongside brand-new 'Brush 2' D5528, while Britannia No. 70036 *Boadicea* waits to depart for Norwich.

'The future is slower than you think.' H class 0-4-4T No. 31551 provides assistance to an outbound service as it climbs out of London Victoria in 1959. Entering service in 1905, it would continue to report for duty until January 1964.

ever-increasingly felt. You can't know that there'll be just as many comparatively new diesels as comparatively new steam engines on the scrap lines by 1969, can't know that a member of Marples' committee will replace Robertson and go on to lead BR in a controversial, divisive and – some would say destructive – way. And perhaps it was better that way. Besides, it was Christmas time. More importantly, it was breakfast time, and as you await the arrival of bacon, egg, sausage and tomato, you turn to the document on the table in front of you. The *Western Region Magazine* always had something good in it, though this number's tinged with just a little sadness for you. There's a competition to name what will be the last steam locomotive to be built for BR. It won't be a King. It won't be a Castle. It won't even be a County. It'll be one of those untidy looking Riddles 9Fs. What would Dad have said? Still, if there has to be a 'last one', you can't help feeling glad it's to be built at Swindon. Your Swindon. Home of some of the finest locomotives ever built, home of the Great Western. Which it still is, as far as you're concerned.

As you wait, you start to wonder. What would *you* call the last steam locomotive? Something with dignity, but finality? Something like 'Evening Star', perhaps?

Yes, perhaps...

Above: Former gas turbine locomotive No. 18100 was re-born as 25 kV electric E1000. Renumbered E2001 in 1959, it is seen here on a passenger working at East Didsbury.

Below: A vision of the future: E3001 was the first electric locomotive to be built specifically for the West Coast Main Line. It was one of twenty-five similar locomotives built by the Birmingham Carriage & Wagon Company, using Associated Electrical Industries equipment. This image is from a special booklet AEI produced in December 1959 to herald their coming.

Above: The new order at Paddington, in the form of Warship D802 *Formidable*, a locomotive whose own eventual 'non-standard' status would see it withdrawn within ten years.

Below: The wheels, if not of industry, then of the railway at least. Here at Swindon Works, the last steam locomotive to be built for BR will take shape. The story continues in *The Sixties Railway*.

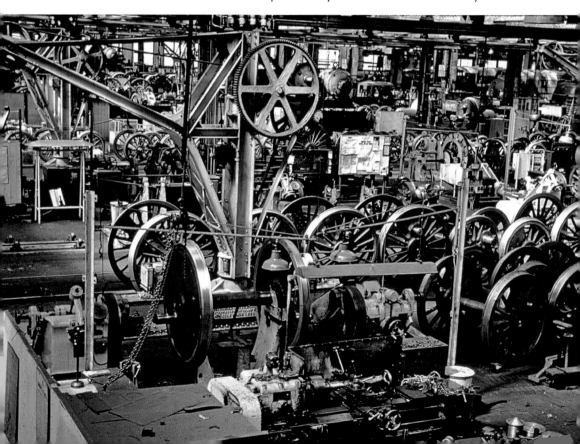

8
What Now?

Reading and Viewing

This book is intended to be a summary of British railway history in the 1950s and is not, therefore, an exhaustive survey. More detailed information may be found in the following volumes:

Bonavia, Michael R., *British Rail: The First 25 Years* (David & Charles, 1981)

Boocock, Colin, *Spotlight on BR: British Railways 1949–1998 – Success or Disaster?* (Atlantic, 1998)

Elliot, Sir John (with Michael Esau), *On and Off the Rails* (George Allen & Unwin, 1982) – includes an account of the Harrow & Wealdstone accident.

Gourvish, T. R., *British Railways 1948–73: A Business History* (Cambridge University Press, 1986) – essential reading for all students of the railway.

Hardy, R. H. N., *Steam in the Blood* (Ian Allan, 1971) – growing up with steam, working with steam and keeping steam going during the era of modernisation.

Haresnape, Brian, *British Rail 1948–1978: A Journey by Design* (Ian Allan, 1979) – covers the design development of locomotives, rolling stock, coach interiors, uniforms, ferries, stations, typefaces and so on.

Johnson, John and Long, Robert A., *British Railway Engineering 1948–80* (Mechanical Engineering Publications Ltd, 1981) – the engineering story, told by engineers and verified by those who were actually there.

Wolmar, Christian, *Fire and Steam: A New History of the Railways in Britain* (Atlantic Books, 2007) – sets the 1950s in the wider rail history context.

The British Film Institute has released a number of British Transport Films' finest documentaries on DVD, including those mentioned in this book, like *Elizabethan Express* and *A Future on Rail*. They are available from a variety of online and high street stores. Other films available on DVD include:

The Titfield Thunderbolt (1953) – the story of a successful attempt to save an idealised branch line (see page 24).

The Ladykillers (1955) – includes several railway scenes shot in the King's Cross area.

Web Resources

The National Archives: www.nationalarchives.gov.uk The National Archives – formerly the Public Record Office – has an online catalogue, listing its collection of official and business-related documents. Copies of some items may be ordered through the site. Visits may also be arranged.

The Railways Archive: www.railwaysarchive.co.uk Most of the source documents referred to in this book – including the reports on the Harrow & Wealdstone (1952) and Lewisham (1957) accidents – may be downloaded free of charge from this important online resource.

RailServe: www.railserve.com This is a comprehensive guide to 19,000 railway websites and upcoming events. It features 180 categories, spanning railway travel, railway enthusiasm, and the railway industry.

Search Engine: www.nrm.org.uk/researchandarchive The National Railway Museum has an extensive online library and archive. Catalogues list details of the museum's extensive collection of papers, drawings, reports, timetables, photographs and so on. Copies of many items can be ordered through the site.

Museums

Barrow Hill Roundhouse Railway Centre, Campbell Drive, Barrow Hill, Chesterfield, Derbyshire, S43 2PR. Telephone: 01246 472450. Website: www.barrowhill.org *Britain's only surviving, operational roundhouse engine shed.*

Crewe Heritage Centre, Vernon Way, Crewe, Cheshire, CW1 2DB. Telephone 01270 212130. Website: www.creweheritagecentre.co.uk

National Railway Museum, Leeman Road, York YO26 6XJ. Telephone: 01926 621261. Website: www.nrm.org.uk

'Locomotion', the National Railway Museum at Shildon, Shildon, County Durham, DL4 1PQ. Telephone: 01388 777999. Website: www.nrm.org.uk/PlanaVisit/VisitShildon.aspx

Heritage Railways

Bo'ness & Kinneil Railway, The Scottish Railway Preservation Society, Bo'ness Station, Union Street, Bo'ness, West Lothian EH51 9AQ. Telephone: 01506 822298. Website: www.srps.org.uk/railway.

Great Central Railway, Loughborough, Leicestershire LE11 1RW. Telephone: 01509 230726. Website: www.gcrailway.co.uk. *The only double track heritage line in Britain.*

Isle of Wight Steam Railway, The Railway Station, Havenstreet, Isle of Wight PO33 4DS. Telephone: 01983 882204. Website: www.iwsteamrailway.co.uk. *Experience Island rail travel as it was before many lines were closed and Tube trains took over the Ryde–Shanklin route during 'The Sixties Railway'.*

Llangollen Railway, The Station, Abbey Road, Llangollen, Denbighshire LL20 8SN. Telephone: 01978 860979. Website: www.llangollen-railway.co.uk. *Operates a variety of steam and diesel locomotives, along with several 'first generation' diesel multiple units.*

The Midland Railway, Butterley Station, Ripley, Derbyshire DE5 3QZ. Telephone: 01773 747674. Website: www.midlandrailwaycentre.co.uk. *The Midland Railway Trust's large collection includes many diesel locomotives and multiple units from the BR era.*

Nene Valley Railway, Wansford Station, Stibbington, Peterborough PE8 6LR. Telephone: 01780 784444. Website: www.nvr.org.uk. *Home to some diesel locomotives and has plans to create a 'travelling post office' museum.*

North Yorkshire Moors Railway, 12 Park Street, Pickering, North Yorkshire YO18 7AJ. Telephone: 01751 472508. Website: www.nymr.co.uk.

Swanage Railway, Station House, Railway Station Approach, Swanage, Dorset BH19 1HB. Telephone: 01929 425 800. Website: www.swanagerailway.co.uk. *Home to many Bulleid Pacifics.*

West Somerset Railway, The Railway Station, Minehead, Somerset TA24 5BG. Telephone: 01643 704996. Website: www.west-somerset-railway.co.uk. *26-mile heritage line through the Quantocks.*

Strathspey Railway, Aviemore Station, Dalfaber Road, Aviemore, PH22 1PY. Telephone: 01479 810725. Website: www.strathspeyrailway.co.uk. *Steam and vintage diesel through the Highlands from Aviemore to Boat of Garten.*

Many of Britain's heritage railways use locomotives, rolling stock and infrastructure that were built, manufactured or used throughout the 1950s. Some even host themed events around the era, details of which may be found in various books and magazines, as well as the Heritage Railway Association website: www.heritagerailways.com.

Getting Involved

There are many railway societies, model railway societies and preservation societies in Britain. Here is just a small selection of some of the more general ones:

The Electric Society (www.electric-rly-society.org.uk) caters specifically for those interested in electrified railways across the world. It holds regular meetings in London and Birmingham.

The Historical Model Railway Society (www.hmrs.org.uk) was founded in 1950 by historians and modellers to collect and exchange records, drawings and photographs in the interests of historical accuracy in modelling. With around 2,000 members worldwide, it remains strongly committed to gathering and distributing UK railway information. It has a large collection of photographs and drawings, a large library and has published a series of definitive books, largely concentrating on railway liveries.

The Railway Correspondence and Travel Society (www.rcts.org.uk) caters for people interested in all aspects of railways past, present and future. It publishes a monthly magazine – *The Railway Observer* – organises local meetings, has a lending library open to members and produces books of enviable accuracy.

The Signalling Record Society (www.s-r-s.org.uk) maintains and shares knowledge of railway signalling and operation in Britain and overseas. It publishes books and possesses much archive material, including photographs and drawings which may be purchased. Modern material is being added to the digital archive regularly. Members are able to download some of the digital material free of charge.

Experiences and Volunteering

Heritage railways are only really possible because of the huge volunteer workforce that helps keep them running. From cooks to cleaners, drivers to guards, signal staff to station masters, most will be giving up their spare time to work gratis in an environment they love. If you are keen to join in, it is best to contact your chosen heritage line direct. For non-safety related roles, basic training will probably be provided, but anything involving the movement of trains is likely to require more rigorous preparation, testing of one's understanding of operating rules and so on.

If, however, the experience of driving a train is sought on a more informal basis, many short courses are available which allow members of the public to drive a steam or diesel locomotive. Again, contacting individual heritage lines direct (via their websites) is the most effective way to find the right course for you.

Collecting

Railways were veritably made for collecting, from large items like locomotive nameplates – some of which can run to thousands of pounds – to smaller pieces like clocks or watches. For the larger ephemera, specialist auction houses (like Great Central Railwayana Auctions – www.gcrauctions.com) are recommended, though you can start a collection of tickets, timetables or postcards, say, by visiting car boot sales, model railway exhibitions or any online auction site. Many railway enthusiast magazines include features on recent sales and high-value items of interest.